Inspections Small and Medium-Sized Businesses

My Experiences

Promote Loss Control...
Attract Customers

Written by: Meg Lee

ISBN: 978-1-4834-3645-6 (sc)
ISBN: 978-1-4834-3644-9 (e)

Because of the dynamic nature of the Internet, any web addresses or links contained in this book may have changed since publication and may no longer be valid. The views expressed in this work are solely those of the author and do not necessarily reflect the views of the publisher and the publisher hereby disclaims any responsibility for them.

Lulu Publishing Services rev. date: 12/21/2015

Contents

Intent

Remember the compliment you received about the service or work you provided? Did the message positively motivate you?

The fact that you are reading this page indicates you value time and may be interested in absorbing condensed information about inspections.

Before the phone rings regarding a commercial inspection, I encourage you to take some time to read this handbook. The intent is for you to regard the material as tips for promoting loss control philosophies while attracting valuable customers.

This handbook focuses on my experiences with commercial inspections, especially insurance assessments. The information emphasizes organization, reducing hazards and positively enticing others to your business so services or goods will be purchased.

The notations, data and concepts in this handbook are only helpful suggestions and outlines. Utilizing the information holds the writer, M. E. Lee (a.k.a. Meg Lee) harmless. These ideas are based upon general evaluations and not replacements for current state and federal laws, regulations or other requirements.

Approach and How this Handbook Can Help You

Suggestion read **Part I,** in addition to the chapter or chapters applicable to the business or businesses you own, manage or are interested in. Bear in mind that the inspector may become your customer or can refer someone to you. Therefore, during the entire inspection process it is good to project professionalism and a willingness to work things out.

Once contacted, verify the name of the company for whom the examiner is conducting the inspection for. Insurance and other companies request inspections to clarify facts and for safety reasons.

Typically, inspectors look at what surrounds the property then review the interior aspects of the structure. During this process, digital photos are taken, observations are made and questions are asked.

Knowing specifics about the information inspectors obtain may also help, if you are considering renting or purchasing commercial property. Other data may prompt you to refine aspects of a business plan or this handbook may provide useful outlines to the delegated person handling your office and safety matters.

If you purchase the paper version of this handbook, use the space at the end of applicable pages to enter specific information about your property and business operations.

Approach and How this Handbook Can Help You

The following are important characteristics that can direct your thinking about property.

- Location
- Construction
- Functionality

In addition, it is a good idea to obtain documentation regarding the construction materials used to create the building you have or are thinking about renting, leasing or buying.

As such, knowing what the roof, ceiling, walls, flooring and foundation of a building consist of is important.

On the other hand, regardless of what your specialties are, direct eye contact, friendly exchanges and a sincere interest to be of service to others are welcome expressions!

The light is on inspections.

Therefore, with so many to embrace ... Keep your premises clean, organized and safe. (COS).

After all, we are only temporary protectors of this fabulous ... landscape.

Digital Photos

- Often the photos taken by an inspector include photos of the front of the building along with any other structures to the left or right of the business. At least 1 photo is typically taken far enough away to include all properties.

Other Photos Often Include:

- An exterior front photo of the building only, plus a photo to include the front door and the address.
- Photos of both the left and right side of the building and the back of the structure. Any trees, branches or debris that either are too close to the roof lines or can become some type of problem are other photos taken, as well. (Trees next to the building may have branches touching the structure which rodents or other small animals may use as gateways to climb onto or into your property).
- A photo of the parking lot near the business and any cracks, holes or hazardous areas in the parking lot.

Digital Photos

- A photo of the interior of the circuit breaker panel or box is helpful and this system may be located on the exterior or interior of the building.
- Interior photos are needed of any areas that may cause hazardous issues, trip and falls or other types of injuries. (To elaborate, photos that are taken include ceilings that appear soiled, dangerous work areas, unsanitary conditions, exposed, open-ended wires and extension cords or power surge protectors that are overused. Photos are also taken of cluttered, messy and unorganized units or sections of spaces within a business).

Exterior Surroundings, Roofs and Walls

It is common for the interview and inspection to be completed in a systematic manner.

The inspector may be instructed to notice the areas next to the building and other structures as well as gas stations or other potential hazards nearby. The distance to the closest fire hydrant and fire department is often noted and he or she may look for a fire department connection outside of the building.

Other facts often needed include the condition of the surrounding buildings, the parking lot and the age of the building being inspected.

In addition, is the trash in the dumpster contained or is it overflowing?

Furthermore, the square footage of the building and the square footage of the space you use is typically recorded along with the construction materials used for the roof and outside walls.

It's more important for you to know the types of facts gathered and questions asked so you may quickly use this information to your advantage as opposed to providing specifics regarding the definition and terminology of construction classes. Therefore, details about construction classes are not discussed.

Exterior Surroundings, Roofs and Walls

By the way, a pole camera can be a good tool to use when you need to see what is on a roof.

Some basic, common exterior construction types for roof coverings and walls of buildings are listed next.

- Some roofs may have an exterior covering made of rolled asphalt, rubber membrane or tar and gravel. Otherwise, the cover may be made of metal, wood shingles or tile. Underneath the exterior portion of the roof laminated wood, steel beams or trusses may be seen. (If there is a ladder attached to the exterior side of the building is it easy for vandals to climb onto the roof)?
- Classic wood frames and metal roofs (Common For Storage Facilities)
- Concrete block or masonry type walls
- Brick, stone or stucco veneer walls
- True brick exterior walls
- Concrete block walls, stone or other non-combustible material
- Light metal exterior siding and roofing
- Stucco exterior walls with 1 or more concrete walls
- Hard Stucco or EIFS
  Exterior Insulation and Finish System
  (EIFS seems soft compared to hard stucco).

Interior Roof Frameworks, Walls and Flooring

The inspector also needs to know the composition of the interior roof, walls and flooring in order to determine the construction class.

In addition, is there interior access to the exterior portion of the roof and if yes is the access to the roof unobstructed? Is the access locked when not in use and if yes how is it kept locked? Who manages this access to the roof? Is there anything on the roof such as an air conditioning system? (Please also refer to the prior section regarding exterior construction to read about various types of roof coverings).

- Some interior roof frames are all or partially constructed of wood or another combustible substance.
- Others may be constructed entirely of metal panels.
- Otherwise, it may be a non-combustible material with steel frames that are not fire proof.
- The framework of a roof may include concrete and reinforced steel bars.
  (This may be easier to see if the building is still under construction).

Interior Roof Frameworks, Walls and Flooring

- A roof that consists of concrete and steel framework needs a lot of support and the construction works well when concrete floors, walls and roof form a solid shell.
- Also, walls might be made of wood, other combustible substances, metal panels, stone or a combination of materials.
- The flooring may be raised wood or other combustible materials, tile or concrete applied on the earth or concrete on fire proof steel.

Operations

It is important to have a complete, concise description of your operation readily available. This should include the exact name and address of the business, the number of owners and employees along with their titles, how long the business has been in existence and what type of business it is. (Sole proprietor, Partnership, LLC or Corporation). State how many employees are full time and part time and if any are under the age of 18. In addition, state the hours of operation, services and/or goods offered and who your customers are. Explain how and where the services and/or goods are provided and distributed as well as what inventory is stocked and the approximate value of the inventory. Also, list equipment and vehicles you own, lease or rent for your business and mention if you own, lease or rent the building or space where your business is conducted.

Maintain a record of the amount of annual sales produced for each service, good or product.

Finally, list the name of your website if you have one as well as the past annual net income and your projected annual expenses and gross income.

Organization and Other Considerations

What you place or will maintain in each office and all the rooms of your business is vital. Consider preparing a simple diagram of your facility or, if you are renting space that is part of a building, request a copy of the building floor plan and your unit from the property owner. Make at least 1 copy of this and on the other page document the position of the main contents of each room, for your reference.

It can be very beneficial if an office or offices with expensive computer or other equipment and locked cabinets containing important documentation remain in rooms with no windows or in rooms with windows on a 2nd floor or higher to deter vandalism and theft.

For many types of businesses, a few people or at least 2 people need to have access to the keys to your office or offices, the alarm system, specific locked cabinets and computer passcodes for various important confidential and financial records.

Another idea is to use an external hard drive or an extra laptop computer as a back up to maintain valuable information as opposed to storing everything in an electronic cloud. In addition, consider placing this external hard drive or laptop in a concealed safe at night.

Organization and Other Considerations

Of course, shredding and recycling unnecessary paper each week reduces clutter and confusion.

Compile and concisely organize information about employees, equipment, facts, fixtures, furniture, inventory, necessary protective clothing, property and supplies. Electronic records or scanned documents are great if separately stored copies are kept, yet some paper information usually must also be retained.

Documentation regarding employees, especially information containing social security numbers and addresses, should always be maintained in locked cabinets as should important financial documents that are in hardcopy form.

Furthermore, it is best if water heaters are located on concrete floors, away from everything else and in a separate room so that it may easily be moved and replaced.

If at all possible, circuit breaker boxes should be on a concrete or stucco wall that includes nothing else or far away from anything else.

Verify that cords and other things are not in the paths where people walk so trip and fall accidents are avoided.

Organization and Other Considerations

Hanging wires, exposed open ended wires and extension cord overuse can be very dangerous and should be eliminated. Panel boxes need covers; not including any is hazardous. Temporary light fixtures applied to a pole or something via duct tape are great concerns as well. Permanent, operational light fixtures are a must; flashlights are a good backup.

To eliminate corrosion, store a few flash lights with no batteries inside a drawer and keep extra batteries by the flashlights so these can be added, when needed.

Also, consider having an attorney provide you with a legal, written opinion of your business including agreements or contracts you ask others to sign as well as the services, products or goods you are selling.

Offering food, products and/or services via clean and orderly buildings, units, work areas, cabinets and computer systems makes it easier to conduct business, locate records and details. In fact, this type of environment can bring smiles, peace of mind and happiness.

Offices for Multiple Purposes

Besides the information referenced in the description of operations section, such as the services, products, hours of operation and type of business you own or manage, the inspector may need to ask the following questions.

- Does your business have the necessary documentation to legally operate in this city and state?
  (Examples are a business tax license and an Employer Identification Number, EIN).
- Also, what documentation is given to each customer?
- Do you maintain a record of all income and expenses?
- Have you experienced any problems with the office space? (If yes, what)?
- How long are records pertaining to the business retained?
- How many years have you been at this location?
- Do the lights work and is there enough light?
- Is the entire building locked and are all the windows closed when no one is there?

Offices for Multiple Purposes

- Are all keys kept in a safe or secure metal box or drawer, when not in use?
- Is space rented to others?
- If yes, what for and are agreements and certificates of insurance obtained from the renters?
- If you have employees, is training provided to employees?
- If yes, what training is given?
- Is documentation retained regarding this?
- What special certifications have employees completed?
- Is the documentation regarding this available?
- If needed, will you submit this information?
- Are all employee records, financial data and important information kept locked up when not used?
- Are all records stored at this location?
- If some records are stored elsewhere, where are these maintained?

Utility Systems and Piping

Does the business have the following and if yes, is the system operational or problematic?

- Air conditioner (s)?
- Circuit breaker panel or box with cover?
  Does the wiring, that is seen on the exterior area of the panel or box, involve conduit or BX wiring (armored cable)?
- Heat?
- What type of heating system do you have? (Electrical, Etc.)
- Plumbing?
- Do you see PVC piping near the drainage systems or is there any copper piping anywhere?
- Does the water run freely through all faucets?
- Is there a water heater?
- If there is a water heater is it strapped to the wall?
- Is there some space between the water heater and the wall?
- Is the installation tag attached to the water heater and if yes, is the date it was installed documented?

Safety, Security, Fire Protection and Health Issues

- Does the company have a Safety Manager or Director?
- Are the lights operational and sufficient?
- Is there an emergency lighting system?
- Are periodic safety meetings conducted?
- Are records kept regarding the safety meetings and everyone who attends?
- If you have employees, are they required to wear protective clothing?
- If yes, what clothing or accessories must be worn?
- Is safety literature given to employees?
- Are accident reports kept at this location?
- Are tools and equipment well maintained?
- Are there records which prove the condition of the equipment?
- Have any recent accidents happened due to equipment malfunctioning?
- Will necessary changes be made to increase safety, if the insurance company advises the owner to do so?
- Are the premises of this business shared with a gas station?
- Are there any underground tanks on the premises?
- Are any gas or propane tanks on the premises, if so why?
- If yes, how and where are these stored?

Safety, Security, Fire Protection and Health Issues

- Are guns or firearms kept on the premises?
  (If yes, do you have documentation that legally permits this)?
- How are the windows protected?
- Does anyone reside on the premises of this business? (If yes, who and why)?
- Has there been none, some or a lot of crime in the area in the last 3 years?
- Are there slip or trip and fall hazards, anywhere? (If yes, what and where)?
- How many claims have been submitted in the last 3 years?
- Is it easy to walk around inside the building?
- Is there an operational alarm system at this location?
- When were the fire extinguishers last serviced?
- Are the fire extinguishers properly mounted on the walls?
- How many fire extinguishers do you have?
- What type of fire extinguishers do you have? (Class A, B, C, D or K)
- Is there a sprinkler system?
- Are there smoke detectors?
  (When were these last serviced)?
- Are smoke detectors battery operated?
  (If yes, how often are batteries changed)?

Safety, Security, Fire Protection and Health Issues

- Do you see any soil marks on the ceiling, inside the building?
- Do all exits have illuminated Exit signs?
- Are all exits and door ways unobstructed?
- How many exits are available?
- Is an easy to follow evacuation plan advertised somewhere inside the premises?
- Are applicable state and federal employee regulations posted?
- What type of locks are on the doors?
- Are all the windows to the building and your office closed and are all the doors securely locked when your space is unoccupied and at night?
- Are push bars or "panic hardware" required on any of the doors?
  (These are often in banquet halls, educational facilities or places where numerous people congregate).
- Are the restrooms extremely clean?
- Is there enough toilet paper?
- Does the room have paper towels or hand dryers that work?
- Is there a GFCI with a test button?
  (Ground Fault Circuit Interrupter)
  (Look at outlets near water faucets).
- Is documentation retained regarding Health Department visits and permits?

Stairs, Stairwells and Elevators

- If the office or building has stairs, photos of the stairways are often taken.
- How many stories is the building and how many stories have stairs?
- If there are 4 or more stories is there a floor sign on each landing stating what floor you are on?
- If there are signs, photo 1 sign.
- If there are 4 or more steps, is there a hand rail on both the left and right side?
- Are the stair handrails or guardrails completely secured to the ground or wall and easy to grasp? (Are any damaged)?
- Are there any boxes or items on or near any step that could cause trip and fall accidents? (If yes, please photo these steps).
- What are the steps a.k.a. risers made of? (Concrete, Stone, Wood)
- Are any steps chipped, cracked, damaged or deteriorating?
- Are the steps or risers of uniform height? (In other words, is the height of each step the same)?
- If there is rubber matting on each step is it securely fastened to each step?
- Are there guard rail balusters?
- If yes, is there less than 4 inches of space between each baluster?

Stairs, Stairwells and Elevators

- Is there a document posted in or near the elevator stating information about the certificate?
- What is the date when the elevator was last inspected?
- Is the flooring or ground flush when the elevator door is opened?
  (Once elevator doors are opened, the floor of the elevator and the area outside of the elevator must be completely parallel, even and with virtually no gaps, to help prevent trip and fall accidents).

Apartments

- Who manages the property or what is the name of the management company?
- Is there a sign in front of the building that includes the name and address of the property?
- Is the building in a gated community or is access open to the public?
- Is there a parking lot?
- If yes, does the lot include lined spaces with cement tire stops?
- Overall, how does the condition of the building appear? (Good, Fair, Poor)?
- Is there paint cracking or peeling? (If so, where)?
- Is there enough exterior lighting?
- Are the pathways to each unit clear and cared for?
- Are the grounds well maintained or do the shrubs, trees and plants appear discolored, need trimming or should some or most be removed?
- Is there any sign of water leaks anywhere? (If yes, where)?
- Can mold be seen, if yes where?
- Can you smell any foul orders?
- Is trash contained in dumpsters with lids that completely enclose the trash?
- Are the utility systems, such as the circuit breaker box kept in a locked room? (Please photo this room or area).

Apartments

- Is there a laundry room?
  (If yes, is a key required to enter the room)?
- State the condition of the washers and dryers and note how the floor and ceiling appear. (Photo the room).
- Is there a club room and if yes, note the appearance of it as well as how the exterior and interior walls and ceiling look.
- Is there a pool?
- If yes, is it enclosed by a fence?
- How does the gate close?
- Are safety rules posted?
- Photo the pool area.
- Verify with management that the pool and/or spa drains have anti-entrapment drain covers.
- Is there a life ring and shepherd's hook mounted on a wall and are these easily seen and accessible?
- What is the depth of the pool?
- Does it include a diving board?
- Are there any exterior balconies to any of the units?
- If yes what, if anything is on the balcony or balconies?
- Are renters prohibited from placing and using grills on the balconies?

Apartments

- If there are stairwells and hallways, photo a representative sample of these.
- Do the hallways and stairwells have enough light? (Refer to the section regarding stairs).
- Do the hallways have cement flooring?
- Otherwise, what is the construction of the flooring near the door to each apartment?
- How many fire extinguishers are there and are all properly mounted on the hallway walls?
  (Note the date these were last serviced).
- Photo the mailbox and lobby area (s).
- How many floors and apartments are there?
- Does every unit have a direct exit to the outside of the building?
- Is an emergency lighting system installed?
  (If yes, where)?
- Are any apartments currently vacant?
- If so, how many?
- Are any apartments ADA compliant?
- Have there been any evictions in the last 3 years?
  (If yes, how many)?
- Which units were impacted by evictions?
- Are the agreements that renters sign for 1 year, 6 months or monthly?

Apartments

- Is there documentation within each agreement that requires the signer to keep the space clean, well maintained and to report in writing any problems or damages as soon as possible?
- Is there a clause in each agreement that states that the monthly rental amount owed is due by a certain time period each month?
- If yes, what are the terms regarding the rental fee?
- What happens if the payment is late?
- Is a late fee charged?
- What happens if the regular monthly payment and the late fee is not paid within the time period allowed?
- If this type of information exists in each written agreement that is to be signed by a renter, how is it enforced?
- Do you conduct or request a background check on each potential renter before leasing an apartment to someone?
- Are any apartments in need of repairs?
- If yes, which units?

Apartments

- Does each renter have a microwave, refrigerator and stove inside their apartment which they may use?
- If yes, is there documentation available regarding these?
- About what month and year are the microwaves, refrigerators and stoves expected to expire?
- Is air conditioning provided in each unit?
- If yes, approximately what is the age of each air conditioner?
- Before the air conditioners, microwaves, refrigerators and stoves expire, do you plan to make the necessary arrangements to replace these or how do you plan to handle such matters?
- Is there a carbon monoxide detector in every apartment?
- If yes, where is it placed and about how many feet is there between the carbon monoxide detector and the bedroom or bedrooms?
- Does each unit have a smoke detector?
- Do you provide each renter with the replacement batteries for smoke detectors?

Auto Repair Services

- Is there a sign in front of the building that includes the name of the business?
- What services are available?
- Do you refuse to provide certain services? (If yes, what)?
- Do you refuse to service certain types of automobiles? (If yes, what)?
- What documentation is given to each customer and are recommendations provided?
- Do you maintain a record of all repairs, sales and expenses?
- About how many customer cars are left at this business each night?
- About how long are records kept regarding vehicles that were repaired or serviced?
- Are vehicles kept overnight here?
- If yes, are vehicles stored in a building?
- Are vehicles stored outside in a tasteful fenced area? (Stone Fence, Etc.)
- If yes, is the fence locked at night or when no one is at the business?
- Are any of the vehicles stored overnight at another location?
- If so, where are they stored?
- Approximately how many are stored at this other location?
- Are the windows to vehicles rolled up when no one is working on them?

Auto Repair Services

- Is each car to be locked when it is not being repaired?
- Are keys removed from all vehicles that remain at night or are left unattended?
- Are motor vehicle reports requested for each new hire?
- Do you maintain records regarding the inspections completed on your equipment especially those to lift vehicles in the air for close evaluation?
- When were inspections last performed on most of your equipment?
  (Do you have the information that came with the large equipment that is used)?
- Are accident reports kept?
- Are accident facts (if any) reviewed with employees?
- Is a tow truck used in this business?
- If yes, does the company perform contract towing?
- If yes, are the tows incidental matters as these relate to this business?
- If vehicles are towed, how many tow trucks do you have?
- Is there a guard dog on the premises?
- Are vehicles loaned to customers while their vehicle is in your shop for repairs?
- Are vehicles rented or leased to others?
- Is documentation retained regarding permits and inspections?

Auto Repair Services

- Does an employee road test the vehicles after the repairs or services are finished?
- Are employees allowed to take customer cars for personal use?
- Does the company re-tread tires?
- Are the premises of this business shared with a gas station?
- Are there any underground tanks on the premises?
- Are all flammable liquids and paints stored in UL approved cabinets?
- Does this business salvage vehicles?
- Are vehicles dismantled?
- Does this business provide maintenance or repairs to racing vehicles?
- Does this business sponsor racing events?
- Are vehicles repaired in accordance to manufacturer's specifications?
- Does the business sell used parts?
- If yes, do the sales exceed 5 % of annual gross receipts?
- Are approved spray booths used?
- Does this business repair trucks in excess of 40,000 pounds, gross vehicle weight?
- Are automobile frames cut or welded?
- Are trailer hitches installed or serviced?
- Are used tires sold or installed?
- Is propane sold?
  (If yes, do sales exceed 5% of annual gross receipts)?

Auto Repair Services

- Are beverages sold on the premises?
- If yes, do beverage sales exceed 10% of annual gross receipts?
- Are vehicles repossessed?
- Are there No Smoking signs posted where combustibles are stored?
- Describe how oil, solvents and similar materials are disposed.
- How often do you remove oils and solvents from your premises?
- Are fuel containers, paint or oily rags left out in the open?
- Do you see safety glasses anywhere?
- If not ask where these are kept and if employees use these, when needed?
- Do employees wear leather, steel-toed shoes?
- Do employees wear gloves, when needed?
- Is there a sign in front of the work area warning customers to Stay Out, for safety reasons?
- Do you use subcontractors?
- If yes, what do you subcontract?
- If yes, do you require subcontractors to sign a written agreement before conducting business with you?
- If yes, does the agreement include a hold-harmless clause?

Auto Repair Services

- Does the agreement require subcontractors to maintain certain types and limits of insurance?
- Is there an electronic cash register that records the orders and is this where cash and credit card receipts are placed?
- If yes, is there a security camera near the register?
- Are bank deposits submitted daily during the day and never at night?

Manufacturing

- Knowing what surrounds the business is important. (For example, are there other businesses along the sides of your property, any debris or combustible materials)?
- Is there a parking lot?
- If yes, in front of the building are there lined spaces with cement tire stops?
- Is there a sign in front of the business that includes the name and address of the business?
- What do you produce?
- Do large trucks come to your facility to pick up shipment orders or deliver supplies?
- If yes, do the trucks come to a loading dock and if so how many loading docks do you have for this business?
- Where is/are the loading dock (s) located for your business? (Photo the loading dock (s)).
- Is there plenty of space for trucks to enter and exit the loading dock area or open spaces near the building?
- What processes are involved to produce what you manufacture?
- Please describe the various processes.
- What equipment is used to manufacture each product?

Manufacturing

- How often is this equipment that is used in the manufacturing process inspected?
- If the equipment is inspected ask if records are maintained that summarize information regarding the inspections of the major pieces of equipment.
- Do customers come to the business?
- If yes, how many come each month?
- How are orders or purchases submitted to you?
- Do customers come to the manufacturing area?
- If yes, why?
- Do they wear protective gear when in this area? (If yes, what do they wear)?
- Is the work area separated from the rest of the business? (Photo the work area).
- Is there a warning sign before the work area stating that all unauthorized people need to Stay Out?
- Are hazardous materials used?
- If yes, what?
- If yes, how do you store the hazardous material when it is not being used?
- Do you have UL approved cabinets for all flammable and combustible liquids?
  (If yes, photo the area where these are located).

Manufacturing

- How and where are hazardous wastes disposed of?
- List any other dangers or hazards that are involved in the business.
- What else do you do to guard against injuries?
- Do you have any eye wash stations?
  (If yes, photo 1. How many feet is this from the work area that involves hazards)?
- Describe the ventilation in the work area and in this business. (Good, Needs Improvement, Poor, Explain)
- Do you apply labels on the product (s) you manufacture? (If yes, photo a label).
- Do you have a patent (s)?
- If yes, what is/are the patent (s)?
- Is your business involved with installing the product you manufacture?
- If yes, to what extent and how is this accomplished?
- Does your business provide service and repairs to the product you manufacture?

Manufacturing

- How do you package your product (s)?
- Who arranges for the shipping of your product (s)?
- Has any product ever been recalled?
- If yes, please state what happened and if this has been resolved. (If applicable, describe the resolution).
- Do you stock inventory?
- If yes, what and about how much?
- Where is the inventory stocked?
- If any merchandise is located on shelves, are the shelves made of steel?
- What is at the base and underneath each shelf?
- How many inches or feet are there between each aisle?
- Approximately how much space is there between the top of the shelves and the ceiling?
- Are shelves appropriately stocked or are too many goods piled on shelves?
- Are there any back rooms?
- If yes and a back room or rooms includes something besides inventory, what is the space used for?
- What is the appearance of the room or rooms?
- How could the room (s) be improved?

Manufacturing

- Do you use subcontractors?
- If yes, what do you subcontract?
- If yes, do you require subcontractors to sign a written agreement before conducting business with you?
- If yes, does the agreement include a hold-harmless clause?
- Does the agreement require subcontractors to maintain certain types and limits of insurance?

Medical Offices

- Is the name of the medical office along with the suite number, if applicable, posted on the ground floor of the building?
- Did someone greet you at the reception desk?
- Do you see a patient sign-in sheet?
- How does the front office area appear?
- Are the countertops free of clutter?
- Is patient information out of sight?
- Is the area neat and orderly?
- Do any of the computer screens display specific patient information, which is to remain confidential?
- Is the front office staff communicating in a professional manner?
- Is there a lot of chatter among the staff or are they focusing on providing service to the patients?
- What is the appearance of the waiting room?
- Is the furniture functional and professional looking?
- Does any of the furniture appear to be unsuitable?
- Are any of the arms, backs, legs or seat cushions damaged or worn out?
- What year did the service start and are only the services noted in your description of operations provided?

Medical Offices

- Note what services are refused, if any.
- Also, what documentation is given to each patient?
- How many doctors provide services at this location?
- How many years has the person being interviewed worked in this industry?
- How many people have access to the keys to the office and/or building?
- Are all keys kept in a safe or locked box when not in use?
- Are all employee records kept in a locked file, when not in use?
- Do the records include applicable employee licenses and certifications?
- Does the office employ medical coders?
- If yes, are the medical coders professionally certified?
- Where are all patient files maintained?
- Approximately how many patients receive medical services at this office?
- How many employees are part time and how many are full time?
- Are background checks requested or conducted before a person begins working at this facility?

Medical Offices

- Besides small instruments what medical equipment is used at this location?
- Are records kept regarding the condition of the medical equipment?
- Are all employee, financial and important records stored at this location?
- If some records are stored elsewhere, where are these stored?
- Do volunteers work here?
- Are volunteers required to sign an agreement before starting?
- If the insurance company requested a copy of this, will it be provided?
- Is training provided to the volunteers?
- What tasks are the volunteers expected to perform?
- Is an OSHA Manual maintained and if yes, ask if you may see it.
- Is this manual in a clean binder and does it appear organized and professional?
- Approximately how many pages are in this manual?
- Are SDS (Safety Data Sheets) kept? (Previously these were called Material Safety Data Sheets).
- Ask if records are maintained that list all chemicals kept at this office.

Medical Offices

- If yes, do these records reveal when products were disposed of?
- Are employees trained to adhere to safety regulations?
- Is documentation maintained regarding specific training sessions and attendees?
- Are safety inspections conducted on a regular basis?
- Is documentation kept regarding the inspections?
- Are all the floors in the office clean?
- Are all electrical cords out of walkways?
- Are drawers to all cabinets closed?
- How many patient rooms are there?
- Does each room appear clean and not cluttered?
- Can medical instruments or tools be seen?
- If yes how are medical instruments sterilized?
- Is each small instrument packaged separately and thrown out after it is used?
- How often are hazardous wastes disposed of?

Medical Offices

- Is a service hired to pick up and discard hazardous wastes?
- Is there anything that seems amis?
- If yes, what?
- Where in the office is this issue?
  (Describe what you see).
- Are there back office rooms?
- If yes, how many?
- What work is conducted in the back office room (s)?
- Is there a desk or desks in the back office room (s)?
- If yes, what is the appearance of the room (s)?
- Do the billing and coding employees work in a back office room?
- How many billing and coding employees are there?
- Is the desk (s) and room (s) of the billing and coding employees free from clutter?
- Look for and ask to see the current coding and medical terminology books.
- Do you see coding books for the current year and prior year? (CPT, HCPCS & ICD Books)

Medical Offices

- Are the medical billing and coding employees reviewing electronic medical records or Word documents to determine the appropriate codes and costs?
- Are the medical billing and coding employees required to decipher hand written notes the doctor (s) have prepared to determine billing amounts and correct codes?
- Who reviews the medical bills and codes before these are submitted for payment?
- Does the office have a Medical Office Procedure Manual?
- Ask to see the procedure manual, does it include the following information?
- The importance of constantly maintaining confidentiality and effective communication.
- The need to provide an extremely neat and professional office.
- The main requirements for all the different positions.
- The importance of documenting facts and only objective statements in a medical record.
- Forms for patients to sign.
- What to do in certain emergency situations.

Medical Offices

- Are Workers' Compensation records separated from other files?
- Is legal correspondence kept in separate files?

Mercantile Stores

- Is there a freeway close by?
- Can you see the building for this business from the freeway?
- Is the store by a frontage road and a freeway?
- Is there a sign stating the business name that can be read from the freeway?
- Does this business have a parking lot?
- If yes, about how many customer parking spaces are there?
- Does each space include the name of the business?
- Is the available parking in an open lot?
- If yes what is the surface of the parking lot? (Asphalt, Cement, Dirt, Stone)
- If the surface is asphalt or cement are the spaces clearly marked and divided by straight lines?
- Does the parking lot have cracks, pot holes or a deteriorating appearance?
- Does each space have a cement tire stop?
- Is the store in a strip mall?
- Note any problems or potential hazards surrounding the business.
  (Look on the left and right sides as well as the back of the structure).
- Is there a sign near the street that states the business name?

Mercantile Stores

- If yes, is the business sign easy to see and read and does it appear in good condition?
- Is the name and street address clearly marked on or near the front door of the store?
- Does the store have any large windows on the ground level?
- If yes, are any damaged?
- Are the windows clean?
- Photo any utility systems near the building. (Circuit Breaker Boxes, Utility Company Units, Etc.)
- Do you see any signs regarding the type of alarm system used? (The name of the alarm company may be listed on a sign).
- Did anyone positively greet you soon after you entered the store?
- Quickly look around the entire interior and document how it appears.
- If there are signs posted, are these professional and easy to read?
- What services or products are offered?
- Are there any displays filled with goods for customers to see?
- If yes, about how much space is between each aisle in the store? (Is there 36 inches or more)?

Mercantile Stores

- Do you stock inventory?
- If yes, what and about how much?
- Where is the inventory stocked?
- If any merchandise is located on shelves, are the shelves at the store made of steel?
- What is at the base and underneath each shelf?
- How many inches or feet are there between each aisle?
- Approximately how much space is there between the top of the shelves and the ceiling?
- Are shelves appropriately stocked or are too many goods piled on shelves?
- Does the store have any back rooms?
- If yes and a back room or rooms includes something besides inventory, what is the space used for?
- What is the appearance of the room or rooms?
- How could these rooms be improved?
- Is there an electronic cash register that records the orders and is this where cash and credit card receipts are placed?
- If yes, is there a security camera near the register?
- Are bank deposits submitted daily during the day and never at night?

Restaurants

- Is there a parking lot?
- If yes, does it include lined spaces with cement tire stops?
- Is there a sign in front that includes the name and address of the restaurant?
- Is there a handicap ramp in the front of the restaurant?
- Photo any deteriorating ramps, steps, walkways or parking lot areas.
- Is the front reception area clean and organized?
- In the front or somewhere in the restaurant, is there an electronic cash register that records the orders and is this where cash and credit card receipts are placed?
- If yes, is there a security camera nearby the register?
- Is the furniture in good shape?
- Does any of the furniture appear damaged or unsafe to sit upon?
- Regarding the restrooms, is everything incredibly clean?
- Is there a sign near the sink instructing employees to wash their hands before returning to work?
- Is the floor or tile in the restroom smooth and even?

Restaurants

- Is there a metal bar on the wall, near a toilet that can help a person sit and stand up?
- If yes, is this in a larger restroom stall?
- If yes, does this larger stall have enough room for a person in a wheel chair?
- Are the menus clean and easy to read?
- Is there a dining room with tables and chairs for customers?
- Is the dining room clean and well maintained? (If no, describe it).
- Are the tables without customers, clean?
- Are there any tables and chairs near exits or too close to kitchen doors?
- Is there enough space in each aisle and is it easy to walk in this area?
- Does the restaurant have booths?
- If yes, are any of the booths torn?
- What is the floor covered with? (Tile, Cement, Carpet)
- Are there any trip and fall areas under or near the tables and/or booths? (If yes, please photo this area).
- Is there a sign that states the maximum occupancy for this restaurant?

Restaurants

- What is offered? (Specifically)
- If alcohol is included, ask the next question.
- Does the business have a current liquor license that is applicable for this city and state?
- (Refer to the section on Sports Bars).
- If there is a bar, are all counters and areas behind the bar clean?
- Are all bottles of wine, liquor and glasses appropriately stored and not over stocked?
- If there are any refrigerators in this area are these clean on the exterior and interior?
- How many years have you worked in this industry?
- Is there a fire extinguisher within 30 feet of the kitchen?
- Is the kitchen clean and orderly?
- Are all the appliances cleaned every day?
- Are employees trained on how to store food in the kitchen and refrigerator?
- Are employees instructed on how to set and maintain proper cooking and storage temperatures?

Restaurants

- Are the food prep areas clean and sanitary?
- Do employees wear appropriate plastic gloves when needed?
- Is there a UL 300 compliant wet chemical auto extinguishing system?
- If yes, when was it last serviced?
- When was it manufactured? (After 1994)?
- (If there is a free standing oven or pizza oven, in a very small restaurant an auto extinguishing system (AES) may not be required).
- (A UL 300 compliant, wet chemical auto extinguishing system applies to grease producing cooking appliances).
- Is there at least 1 nozzel from an auto extinguishing system pointed at each grease producing appliance?
- Is there a self-contained cooking unit?
- Are there any deep fat fryers?
- If yes, are these 16 or more inches from open sources of flame or heat?

Restaurants

- If no, is there a stainless steel vertical baffle (barrier) of at least 8 inches in height separating the deep fat fryers from heat sources?
- Does the hood exhaust system have removeable stainless steel baffle grease filters or mesh filters?
- Is there a gutter or metal tray to collect excess grease?
- In the kitchen, are there any items on the ground that may cause trip and fall accidents or other problems? (If yes, describe what you see).
- Is the floor dry in this area with very little or no grease?
- Is there any grease or soiled marks on the walls or ceilings?
- Are bank deposits submitted daily during the day and never at night?

Sports Bars

- Is it easy to exit and enter the parking lot?
- Does the parking lot include lined spaces with cement tire stops? (These can help prevent cars from rolling and causing damage).
- Is there a sign in front of the structure that states the name and address of the sports bar?
- Are any signs posted, such as No Open Container and No Smoking?
- Is there enough exterior lighting?
- Do you see any graffiti or indication that vandalism has occurred?
- If yes, photo the damages.
- Upon entering the bar, do you see a sign that states the maximum capacity?
- Do any of the bar stools appear damaged or worn out?
- Does the business have a current liquor license that is applicable for this city and state?
- Are all counters and areas behind the bar clean?
- Are all bottles of wine and liquor appropriately stored and not over stocked and is the same true for all the glasses?
- If there is a refrigerator (s) in this area are these clean on the exterior and interior?

Sports Bars

- How many years have you worked in this industry?
- (If the bar also has a kitchen and provides food especially hot food, the questions listed via the section regarding Restaurants will also be helpful).
- Are employees trained to identify customers who have had too much to drink?
- If yes, what instructions are given to the employees?
- Do you maintain the information regarding each employee that allows him or her to legally serve alcohol in this city?
- Do you have security guards?
- If yes, how many and when do they work?
- What training have the guards completed?
- Do you obtain a copy of the document that proves when and where the guards have completed the applicable training?
- What entertainment is provided?
- Are there televisions and a pool table?
- Do entertainers sing or perform?
- If yes, approximately when?

Sports Bars

- Do you allow others to use space for events and gatherings?
- If yes, do you request that they sign an agreement?
- If yes, what are the most important clauses in the agreement that protect you?
- Do you obtain certificates of insurance from these performers and others who rent out space?
- If yes, approximately what are the limits of insurance?
- Is there an electronic cash register that records the orders and is this where cash and credit card receipts are placed?
- If yes, is there a security camera near the register?
- Are bank deposits submitted daily during the day and never at night?

Warehouses

- What type of equipment do you use?
  (Forklifts, Etc.)
- If you use forklifts are these powered with gas, propane or operated via portable batteries?
- Does your business require propane tanks and if yes, do you use a service to exchange these?
- If yes, how often and where on the premises are the tanks kept, moved and exchanged?
- Do you keep a record of this information?
- What product or service is stored at the warehouse?
- Describe how the inside of the warehouse appears.
  (Orderly, Messy, Dirty, Etc.)
- Do you stock inventory?
- If yes, what and approximately how much?
- Photo the warehouse and work area.
- Are there shelves inside the warehouse?
- If yes, are the shelves made of steel?
- What is at the base of each shelf?
- Are there wood or metal pallets at the base of each shelf?
- About how much space is there between the top of the shelves stocked with goods and the ceiling?

Vacant Structures

- Is there a parking lot?
- If yes, what condition is it in?
- If yes, are there cement tire stops on all the parking spaces, especially those near the building?
- Ask management if the exterior lights are operational and record the answer.
- Are there any portable exterior lights attached to the building near the roof line?
  (With vacant buildings, it may be very important to view the roof via a pole camera before entering the interior).
- Are there any trees or bushes near the building that appear burned and should these be removed or are there any bushes that need to be trimmed and taken care of?
- Are there any signs posted, such as no loitering or no smoking?
- Is there any indication of vandalism or graffiti?
- Does the foundation and exterior walls of the building have signs of decay or deterioration?
- If yes, what and where?
- Are the doors boarded?
- Are padlocks on the doors?
- What are the exterior doors made of?
- Are any windows broken or damaged?

Vacant Structures

- Do the interior lights work?
- What is the condition of the interior floors, walls and ceiling?
- Photo any area (s) that are in need of repair, such as paint that is peeling.
- Are there any holes in the walls?
- If yes, look inside the holes and note what you see.
- Try to find out why the wall (s) have holes.
- Make sure you have a photo showing the interior of the circuit breaker box.
- Is the ceiling sagging or do you see any holes in the ceiling?
- Does the ceiling have water stains or other damage?
- Is the building empty or are there items inside?
- If it is not empty, list what is inside the building.
- If there are goods or things inside, describe how these look and are being stored.
  (Clean, Dirty, Orderly or Disorganized)
- If the building is empty, describe what can be seen inside and photo the area.
- If possible, photo any unusual issues surrounding or inside the structure.

Warehouses

- Are the entrances and exits large enough for trucks to pass through?
- Are there other businesses or structures next to the warehouse?
- Is there any debris or combustible material outside of the warehouse?
- Is the parking lot small, medium or large?
- Photo several different views of the lot and include any major signs and hazardous areas that may exist.
- Is there plenty of light in the parking lot?
- Verify that you have a photo that includes some of the light poles.
- Confirm with management that the exterior lights are all operational.
- Do all the parking spaces that are close to the building have cement tire stops?
- Is there any indication of vandalism?
- Does the warehouse have loading docks?
- If yes, photo these.
- Do you have bulk storage of flammable liquids ar combustibles?
- If yes, are the flammable liquids kept in UL app cabinets when not used?
- Are No Smoking signs posted?
- If yes, is no smoking inside the premises an building enforced?

Warehouses

- Are the shelves appropriately stocked or are too many goods piled on shelves?
- How many inches or feet are between each aisle way and the next shelf?
- Are there any unusual interior issues?
- If yes please describe what you see and take a few photos, if possible.

Conclusion and Background

If asked to simply describe the strongest attribute of the best services and businesses, I will say it is their GOODWILL that resonates.

While developing or adjusting sensible, economical business plans and before making decisions that impact the property relevant to your business, it helps to understand the commercial inspection process. Therefore, this handbook of information was compiled for you.

During the past several years, I have been conducting commercial inspections. Prior to this and after entering the California insurance services industry in the fall of 1991, the work I performed involved customer service, claims adjusting and arbitration administration.

Additional expertise was gained about hazards and injuries by completing professional credentials such as the OSHA Standards for General Industry, Commercial Inspections and a California Insurance Adjuster's License.

My knowledge revolves around inspection processes, commercial, personal and workers' compensation insurance, medical office procedures and a Bachelor's degree.

Through time and grace ...
You can always refine your place.